JAH REVENGE
BABYLON REVISITED

MICHAEL THOMAS/ADRIAN BOOT

EEL
PIE
PUBLISHING

First published in 1982 by Eel Pie Publishing Limited,
45, Broadwick Street, London W1V 1FS

© Adrian Boot and Michael Thomas 1982

ISBN 0 906008 59 X

The authors would like to thank Lynne, Karen, and
everyone at Island.

The lyrics to *Johnny Too Bad* are reproduced by
courtesy of Blue Mountain Music Ltd.

A Crunch Design.

Printed and bound in Great Britain.

Incident Uptown: Police gun down fugitive.

Claudie Massop never knew what hit him. He'd been out playing football, scored a couple of goals, and he was in a taxi on his way home with a couple of mates and they ran into a roadblock. The police reckoned they found a gun. They probably did. They hauled Claudie and his mate out of the car and put them up against the wall. Then they told the taxi-driver to run, and he didn't need to be told twice, he ran like hell. Shots were fired. When they brought him in, Claudie had half a dozen bullets in his back. You could see the holes under his arms. Not long after, Bucky Marshall ended up face down in a flaky Brooklyn disco. They'd overshot the mark. They'd outlived their usefulness.

For a while there, during the run-up to the 1980 election when things got totally drastic and all hell broke loose on the streets in Jamaica, characters like Claudie and Bucky and Red Tony and Trinity were hot property. Trinity really caught on, he was in the papers every day – one classic shot of Trinity doing what he did best got picked up by Reuter's and syndicated worldwide. And there you had it, the whole kamikaze charisma of the gunman: he's got a gun in each hand, zigzagging down the street, down on one knee Clint Eastwood-fashion, blasting at the rooftops. Mirrored shades, too-tight leisurewear, one eccentric touch – a flannel in his back pocket, like a tennis pro, and one oh so typically Jamaican touch: no socks. In the background, you can see Eddie Seaga. Trinity was Eddie Seaga's bodyguard.

Claudie ran the JLP boys on the street, and Bucky had a lot of sway with Red Tony's PNP boys, and for a while there, the gunmen ran Jamaica.

The guns are quiet now. The dust has settled. The shops are filling up. You can drive whatever car you want, you can bring it in from wherever you want and nobody will give you the third degree about where you got the money. The lights are on in Montego Bay. All is forgiven.

The flights from Miami are filling up. First time tourists testing the water, and up front in business class a lot of half familiar faces – returning residents, the fugitives from the Manley Years. The big spreads on the North Coast that barely ticked over the last five years are getting a fresh coat of paint. The yardboys are chopping back the rampant bougainvillea. The Manley Years are over. In November 1980, two terms after he stormed to power at the head of a mighty host, Michael Manley fell from grace. He lost the bloodiest election in history by a landslide. Everybody breathed a sigh of relief . . .

1974

Spots makes it fours all round. Eli lays a four-deuce,
Rupert polishes off his bottle of Dragon and lays a
four-three. Spots hoists up on his elbow, his last
domino held high above his head and about to mash
up the game, when artful little Musso, that's short for
Mussolini, Musso comes up with the three-deuce that
makes it a key game, six straight and a clean sheet to
him and Eli. Spots snarls. Eli's opening up another
couple of Dragons with his teeth and Musso keeps
rubbing it in, crowing, going *Clean sheet! Clean
sheet!,* and Eli's laughing so hard his eyes are bulging
like bloodshot golf balls and his adenoids are backing
up and threatening to choke him – it's all too much
for Spots to take. He gets hold of a Dragon bottle and
smashes it on Musso's head. These boys have been
playing for a while so there are plenty of Red Stripe
bottles and Dragon Stout bottles lying about, and
before you can say *bauxite!* the knives are out and
Musso's bleeding from the right eye and Rupert's lost
an earlobe, someone knocks out the light and they're
up and running in the dark . . . leaving Musso groping
in the doorway, down on his knees in the scattered
dominoes and broken glass.

Dominoes, you might think, is a kid's game. But
when you're down in the dirt in a backyard in Trench
Town, sitting around in the rising stench with nothing
better to do than hang around all day getting in
each other's way, then the drop of a hat can start a
fight, and anything as fraught with dangerous
competition as a simple game of dominoes can get
quickly out of hand and turn into grievous bodily
harm and malicious wounding. It's – the *pressure.*

There's a lot of deep menacing talk going around
Trench Town about the *pressure.* And not just down
in the stench. Up past Half-Way Tree around the new
supermarket piazzas, all over Kingston, and way up
in the hills on the canefields and five-acre farms

 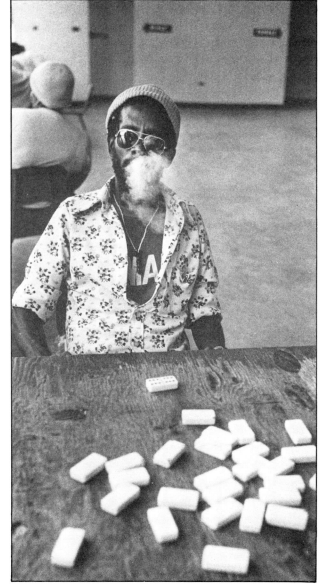

whenever a bunch of Rastas and Rude Boys find themselves in somebody's backyard, taking it easy on a pound and a half of some of the smoothest and most narcotic ganja in the world, what's on their mind all the time these days is the *pressure*. And when some old fiend fuses his synapses on too much white rum and Nutriment and goes out and does the unspeakable to a five-year-old child, everybody round about has a certain amount of sympathy for him, because they know it's not his fault, it's just the pressure got too heavy for him and he couldn't think straight. The poor old boy couldn't help but lash out at the nearest living thing. Everybody's feeling it, and the pressure like some sinister infection keeps on rising with the murder rate. It plays on the paranoia of the merchant classes and the business community locked up in their hilltop villas, with an uneasy eye on the kitchen girl and the kitchen girl's yardboy with the machete. They've got an intercom system connecting them to their neighbours just in case. They're scared stiff, and they have good reason to be. Every night, somebody gets caught in the crossfire – and not just trigger-happy kamikaze kids down in Trench Town either, but prominent taxpayers and friends (and enemies) of the Government, shot from ambush in full view of their wives and children and

not necessarily robbed – till nobody can be sure what's going on any more and everybody dreads to think, is there some kind of diabolical terrorist campaign behind it, or some kind of Sino-Syrian business vendetta, or is it Machiavellian party policy to justify a suspension of civil liberties and the democratic process, or just the first sporadic convulsions of the imminent apocalypse. There are all these people on the streets with sticking plaster on their eyebrows and bandages on their heads. Even the beggars are carrying crowbars.

Babylon on a thin wire, the Rastas say, and what they mean is the whole island, as it struggles to cope with post-colonial adolescence in a world going broke, is threatening to come apart at the seams. There are tanks in the streets of Kingston, and a spot six o'clock curfew in Montego Bay, helicopters with searchlights straffing the shantytowns, paramilitary shock troops charging around the countryside shooting down the ganja planes, grim draconian legislation introducing indefinite detention without trial for anyone found carrying a gun. Wartime measures, these, like Northern Ireland, where there's a war on. There's not supposed to be a war on in Jamaica.

'Soon-come,' says Spots, drawing himself up into his most ferocious posture, nostrils flared, eyes smouldering with righteous anger, like George Foreman putting the evil eye on Joe Frazier – 'Revolution soon-come!' But soon-come is soon enough in Jamaica. Nobody's getting up first thing in the morning and mixing molotovs and sweating over the mimeograph. The revolution Spots has in mind has no such logic – it's a matter of haphazard slapstick violence.

What happens is a couple of Rude Boys like Spots and Rupert go and see a re-run of *Kiss of Death*, to check out the scene near the end where Richard Widmark pushes the old granny down the stairs in her wheelchair – and laughs. That's the part Spots loves, the way Widmark's lips fold back from his gums and he laughs.

They'd go and see *Kiss of Death* and then they'd end up in somebody's yard pie-eyed on too much Red Stripe and ganja. And one minute they're feeling not too bad at all, they're comfortable, and then somebody says something *personal*, and somebody else takes it *personal*, and next thing – *Bloodclaat! Sodomite!* – the knives are out and somebody gets hurt because they're so wired up they've got to take it out on somebody else and it doesn't matter who. The other day, an old man got shot on his doorstep and robbed of his lunch – a couple of sandwiches and a soursop in a brown paper bag. Old Dennis, the Maroon, up on his dasheen patch in the bush outside Moore Town, says the Devil's got into those boys down there. But Ridley, who's younger, in his twenties, and spent six months in a steelworks in Sheffield, says the Devil is only poorness.

They're Christian kids from the country, most of them, who hit West Kingston with high hopes, and all they found were too many people living in oil drums and fruit-crates and one-room plywood outhouses, with nothing inside except a formica dinette and a glass cabinet for the family china and a radio blasting. West Kingston, literally, is a garbage dump. It used to be a fishing village outside town, and then the city started reclaiming the harbour and they turned it into a dump. One day, the Israelites appeared – lost tribes of dirt-poor unemployed, homeless scavengers and vagrant Rastas, all washed up there in the rising stench. They built shacks and huts out of anything they could get their hands on, cardboard and plywood and rusty old iron, and the place spread like a disease till now it's teeming. Kingston itself is in a basin, shut in by the Blue Mountains, and in the summer, when the sun fries the street and the asphalt begins to bubble and erupt and the dirt and zinc-dust and nameless industrial vapours hang in the air, down in Trench Town and Jones Town and Tivoli Gardens and the other shantytowns down in West Kingston, you choke. In the sixties the bulldozers moved in, the town planners chased the squatters off Acknee Walk and put up a few concrete highrises, but already they're falling down and burying whole families alive. West Kingston remains a bombsite landscape of live garbage and boxwood and unlikely tropical greenery.

And still they come to town, gangling teenage runaways from the canefields and five-acre farms, all looking for something faster than chopping cane and humping bananas all their lives. Not sure, most of them, what they're really looking for at all – except they've all seen *The Harder They Come*, they know Jimmy Cliff was just a country boy running with the Rudies until he bluffed his way into Leslie Kong's record store or somewhere with a little tune he'd written. Jimmy's cool, but every Rude Boy on Beeston Street reckons he could do just as good, no trouble at all, and Spots reckons he could probably do better, he could make Jimmy beg.

Just like they reckon if they could just get past the residual colonial élitism of the selectors they could give Lawrence Rowe 25 runs start and beat him to 100, they could get in there first wicket down and knock Thomson and Lillee from here to the Gabba and back.

This, historically, was the reason it was so simple for the shotgun producers like old Leslie Kong to burn the Rude Boys when the whole record business took off in the early sixties. The Rude Boys couldn't care less. They'd never heard about royalties anyway, and they weren't going to sit still to be told. They were glad to grab ten dollars and get back down to Trench Town and put themselves about – they were after the instant Karma. Then a kid like Jimmy Cliff could oh so casually take a pull on his bottle of Red Stripe at the Sound System and ask the brother next to him how he liked the sounds, and when the brother said it was a boss sound, Jimmy could roll his head back and close his eyes for a minute like the tune was really doing him in, and then snap out of it and say, oh so casually: 'That's I singin', y'know' – and crack a big

Perry Henzell.

horrible grin as the brother went green with envy.

That was the pie in the sky. Back in the thirties and forties, before Independence in 1962, Jamaican music was mostly just soundtrack for the swaying palms and silver sands and azure seas – bland and sleek and not too loud, just the speed for the swank resort lounges around Ocho Rios and Montego Bay. There were some suave Latin bands, and there was all that decaffeinated calypso. Calypso, in fact, is the singing journalism of Trinidad, polished, articulate stuff pitched halfway between insolence and insouciance. Jamaican calypso, what's called *mento*, is crude and simple, and back in the fifties the Baptists and the Church of God saw to it that the best *mento*, the lewd stuff, never got far out of the backyard. There was no record industry to speak of.

Down on the street, the kids were listening to the radio, to Fats Domino and Sam Cooke and the Coasters and the Drifters and all that low-rent ghetto rhythm and blues. They weren't allowed in anywhere, they didn't have any money, there was nowhere to go and nothing to do. So when some clever devil got hold of a couple of speakers and a pile of 45's and started running around all over West Kingston and up in the hills putting on backyard disco, Sound System caught on fast.

Soon there were a lot of them, and there still are, travelling deejays piling on more and more wattage and fighting over private stashes of hot 45's, each one trying to blitz out the other. Duke Reid used to arrive at his shows in flowing ermine, a mighty gold crown on his head, a Colt .45 in a cowboy holster, a shotgun over his shoulder and a cartridge belt slung across his chest. He was magnificent, gold rings on every finger and thumb, the dread double-image of Hollywood gangster and high camp aristocrat the Rude Boys go for. He'd have himself carried through the ruck to his turntables. And then he'd let one go, the latest Lloyd Price, a rare old Joe Turner, and while the record played, Duke would get on a mike and start carrying on, hollering 'Wake-it-up! Wake-it-up!' and 'Good God!' and 'Jump shake-a-leg!' and so on, just generally steaming up the atmosphere. It was war. Soon there were all these legendary operators like Duke and Prince Buster and Sir Coxsone and a lot of one-nighters all called King or Count or Pope or something grand like that, all piling on the wattage and voltage till the bass was so powerful you could hear it underwater and they had about as much sheer reverb as the human body can stand without backing up and going out of joint. Then it came down to who had the hottest playlist. In there, when the whole Sound System war peaked in the early sixties, the record business took off. Pirated American pressings with the label scratched off so the competition wouldn't know who it was or where to get it changed hands for twenty dollars a copy. Prince Buster and Duke Reid raced each other back and forth to America looking for scoops. But it was all going so fast, there just wasn't enough product. And around about that time, in the late fifties and early sixties, Elvis joined the army, all those

gutless pansies like Fabian took over, and American pop went limp. So it wasn't long before the Sound System men started getting hold of a one-track or a two-track recorder and making their own stuff. It wasn't hard. Duke was right there in his liquor store, Treasure Isle Liquors, in the thick of downtown Kingston. All the talent he needed was outside the betting shop across the street, hanging out all day with nothing to do.

The Sound System was still packing them in and still does, but the action switched to the record end, and anybody who could come up with the cash for some two-track time and get a record pressed was in business. The talent was lining up. There were Rude Boys and Rastas all over Kingston lining up looking for an opening, and nobody bothered about contracts or royalty statements or anything like that. The producer had it all his own way. He took the risk, he paid the deejays to get it on the radio, he took the credit and he got the money. It was wide-open. It was a lot like the rock and roll game in the ghettoes in the fifties.

It was called *ska*, then. Just a beat, a dead simple nagging upbeat that's so simple only illiterate Jamaicans can play it. The Rolling Stones never get it right. Whatever it's been called, ska, bluebeat, rocksteady, or reggae, Jamaican beat is deceptive, there's more to it than you hear. It's clammy, pelvic, and it throbs like a headache, what old Randy down at Randy's Record Store in Kingston calls gummy, so gummy you could throw it up against a wall and it would stick. It works on the marrow and the membrane.

It takes a while to penetrate the patois, and it's only lately that Bob Marley and the Wailers and Toots and the Maytals have got out of the backyard, but now that reggae has cracked the big charts in America, the record business in Kingston is booming. It's like Nashville down there. Dynamic Sounds started off in a shed and these days it's a vast complex of sixteen-track studios and pressing plants and office space, an autonomous economic republic surrounded by barbed wire and patrolled by armed guards to keep out the hopefuls who still show up every day and climb the walls – looking for an opening.

THE HONOURABLE ROBERT NESTA MARLEY O.M.
1945-1981

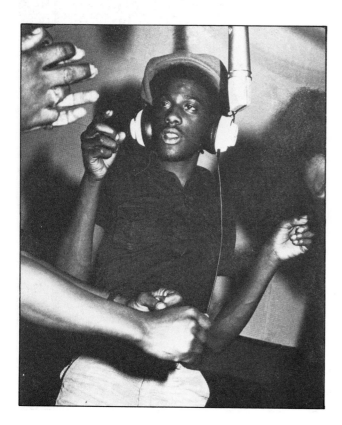

Babylon is on a wire
Babylon is on a wire
An' it's a delicate wire.
An' if JAH, JAH never come 'ere
An' if JAH, JAH never come 'ere
He see I when I pass and gone . . .   Johnny Walker

What they used to do a few years ago, when there were still trams lurching around downtown Kingston at forty and fifty miles an hour, the mad dogs like Spots and Rupert used to play a kind of chicken where they'd wait for a number-nine-tram – that's with the number nine in the speed regulator which meant the driver was drunk with power and in the spirit of the thing and the tram was wound up and going as fast as it could, much too fast, in danger any minute of coming off the rails – and they'd leap on and off at high speed. Tram-hopping it was called. Sometimes they'd hop off one tram on to another one coming the other way, or else there was another manoeuvre where they'd hop on and off and then back on again, just catching the last bar. There was a character called Peter Lorre who won a lot of bets catching the last bar backwards – and he was so deadly cool he held a white rabbit in his arms the whole time. If you missed at forty miles an hour, you'd hit the street and break every bone in your body. A lot of tram-hoppers got mangled pretty badly, quite a few died on impact. That's what made it such a good sport.

These days, now that the trams are gone, the kids go sky-diving on the trains. They get on top of the carriages and gamble on their balance when the train goes down a hill, arms outstretched and legs wide, testing themselves against the updraught, waiting until the last possible second before they duck the overhead viaducts, and then a split second longer, and then – instant Karma.

To prove who can run faster or jump higher or

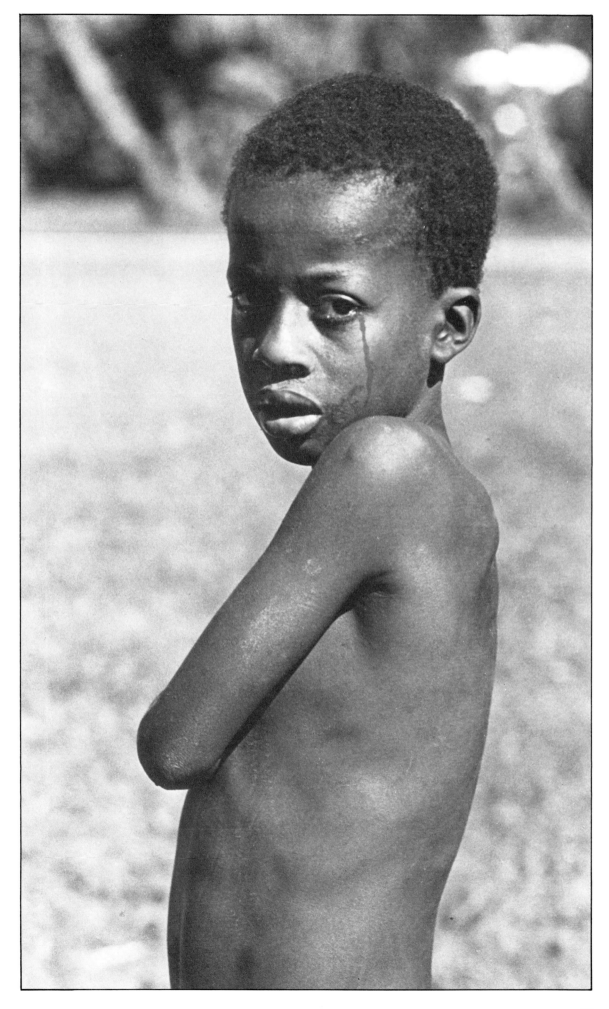

fuck longer or smoke more dope or argue a fine point of natural history with more diabolical cunning and bombast – to stretch your cool and never crack, to the point where you can stop traffic with the sheer authority of your image and kill flies with the ferocity of your concentrated gaze – to be the coolest and deadliest and most debonair Johnny Too Bad on Beeston Street – that's the day-to-day showdown the Rude Boys live for. It's the *pressure*.

They can't get a job unless it's digging ditches, and they're too smart for that. They're too busy thieving and hustling and maybe looking for an opening in the wholesale ganja business, so they can get themselves an S-90, or even a CB-200. Now and then they catch a ride over the mountains to Montego Bay and move a little ganja to the American kids, crush up some Phensic and tell them it's cocaine, perhaps link up with some cockstruck neurotic from New York and take her breath away.

On race days they end up outside the betting shop. Across the street massive battered speakers outside the New York Record Mart will be pumping out the stuff – the reggae. Big Youth and the Heptones and the Wailers and the Maytals and Desmond Dekker, a new one by Burning Spear. And if they've got a horse running out at Caymanas Park and George Ho Sang comes off the bend with a late run, they ride the beast all the way home, snapping their fingers. Not

just a quick little snap, but a vicious whipping crack that takes perfect timing and long loose joints and bony knuckles, so that the fingers hit with the sharp crack of bone splintering . . .

Just the sort of deft digital flourish you need to whip out the blade of a ratchet knife – which is a particular kind of nicely curved blade in a tapered handle, made in Germany for gutting fish. It's a very well-made instrument, dirt cheap at a dollar fifty, and every kid is a master of knife play. They can really perform with a knife. They get their finger in the ring at the end of the handle and snap out the blade so fast it reminds you of that old World War II joke about the Ghurkas – when the German soldier comes face to face with a Ghurka, and the Ghurka whips out his sword and swipes and seems to miss. 'Missed,' says the German. 'Shake your head,' says the Ghurka.

Well, the Rude Boys are faster than that. They make Ghurkas look spastic. They can snap out the blade faster than you can gasp for breath, just to oh so nonchalantly pick a seed out of their teeth or slice off a bothersome hangnail.

Machetes are cheap too – two and a half feet of Sheffield steel goes for less than two dollars. And these are country boys, most of them – if they're not fresh off the canefields their fathers were, and up in the country nobody goes anywhere without his machete in his belt, or dangling from his fingertips,

slapping his leg. Just in case he gets in the mood to clear his dasheen patch, or chop down a couple of coconuts, or just hack away at the nearest tree trunk for no real reason at all, to exercise his arm, perhaps, or test his edge, more often because something comes over him, some sudden incoherent unease, and he feels the need to make his presence felt.

In the daily papers, these days, when the pressure gets too much for some poor fiend and he goes berserk and starts hacking up Violet and Sylvia in their beds, they tend to refer to his machete as a *cutlass*. Which strikes a flamboyant note, recalling the fabulous anarchy of Jamaica's pirate past, when the scourge of the Caribbean operated from Port Royal across Kingston Bay, and the scurviest and most barbarous of them all, Henry Morgan, was knighted by Charles II and made Lieutenant-Governor of the island.

The guns come into the island in different ways. One scandalous story that won't go away insists a lot of them arrived packed into refrigerators during the late sixties and were passed out wholesale by over-eager MPs campaigning in the hills. There is no way of knowing if that's true – there are few facts in Jamaica, only passionate partisan opinions.

They say most of the hand guns – and there are a hell of a lot of them – come in from America in exchange for ganja. Light planes from Florida land in the fields up in the hills, load up with tons of bulging crocus sacks and leave sawn-off shotguns and Colt .45s as part of the deal. That's the official version, but nobody believes that either. All the Too Bad Boys have got a gun, or they can get hold of one as easily as hitting an old man on the head. That makes you a dread man, if you've got a gun. Like Spots' friend Silver Dollar. He just goes by the name Silver Dollar. He goes hauling by, double-clutching down into a 90 degree bend at 65 in his plum-coloured Cortina, which isn't exactly a 30-foot El Dorado with patent leather tyres and Texas longhorns for handles like you see on Seventh Avenue, but he's got tigerfur seat-covers and they cost money. At least it's a car, and any black man with a car's doing all right. 'Him a dread man,' says Spots, as he disappears in a four-wheel drift, sending an approaching schoolbus that's doing about 40 in third on four bald tyres up on to the verge. 'That Silver Dollar,' says Spots, 'him a dread man. Him got a gun, y'know.' *Dread* means a lot. Dread is a word they use in Jamaica when no other word will do, meaning all that is deep and menacing and a threat to body and soul.

In the spring of 1974, so many people were getting shot each day the papers couldn't keep up, and then within a week three big names in the business community got shot. The Government shook with rage. Up in the hilltop villas the middle classes started

An appeal to all citizens of goodwill to help destroy the guns

Take the guns to church.

If you have illegal guns in your possession or know of any —
you're invited by the Minister of National Security and Justice to:-
   leave them in any church hall
   hand them to any Minister of Religion.

Look for the guns.

Search all empty lots and gully courses to locate firearms that have been discarded.
Then phone 119, or report to your nearest police station.
The police will do the rest.

THE GUN COURT ACT STARTS TODAY

THE PENALTY IS INDEFINITE DETENTION

calling Pan Am and getting together on the patio with their neighbours to try and figure out who was next. Manley's Defence Minister, Eli Matalon, threw up barbed-wire compounds like cattle corrals squat in the middle of Kingston. They painted them red because Manley said, 'Red is dread.' He said he didn't like having to go to such lengths, and he hoped everyone would see reason and take their guns to church before the amnesty ended and let the Gun Courts stay empty and rust away. Parsons started getting ammunition clips in their collection bowls, kids found sawn-off shotguns thrown away in the grass. But down in the stench, where the guns are, the pressure backfired. The tanks moved in, and the police charged around busting people on the handy charge of being a suspicious person. The Gun Courts

filled up fast, and when the Privy Council finally ruled indefinite detention unconstitutional, Manley didn't let that stop him, he made it a mandatory life sentence, no appeal. While he was about it, Matalon's successor came up with a new law – what's known as the utterance law, which makes any utterance construed as derogatory or intending to undermine constitutional authority an offence, and bars the felon from ever holding electoral office. Manley said, you have to understand the legislation as part of a total philosophy in relation to crime and punishment.

And all it means is that the pressure is coming down heavier on the Too Bad Boys on the street already on the point of running amuck, and it makes them all the more determined to live fast, die young, and have a good looking corpse.

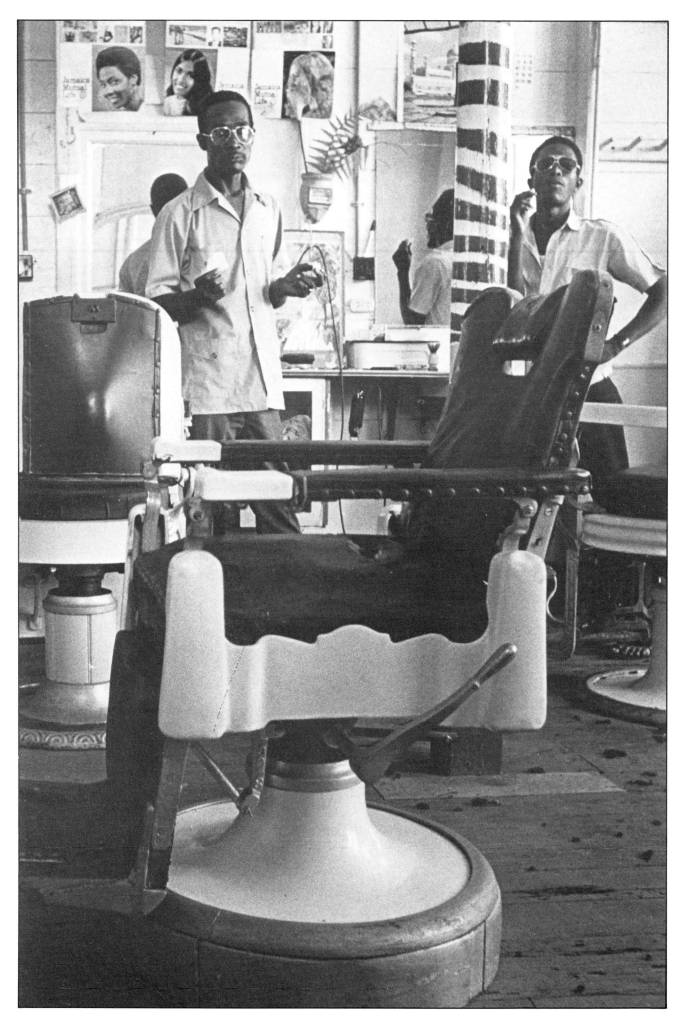

*A couple of years later, by 1976, there was no doubt
about it. The haphazard cowboy violence wasn't so
haphazard, it was being wound up from the sidelines.
The nightly slaughter was the sharp end of the
ongoing political debate. Depending who you
believed, there was a CIA plot to destabilise Manley's
stalled revolution, or else it was a Spassky-like Soviet
stratagem – this took a little longer to get to the point,
but the view taken by the JLP people was that the
KGB had moles in high places, characters like the
shadowy Hungarian in charge of the bauxite
negotiations who seemed a little too nonchalant, all
too willing to run the big ship of the economy onto
the rocks and scare off foreign exchange. Not to
mention all the Cubans all over the place. What
Michael got round to calling democratic socialism
irresistibly conjured up in the venal JLP mind a Cuba-
like one-party state riding roughshod over the private
sector, in other words a knife at their throat. So they
took off. They abandoned their villas to the
bougainvillea and took off before whoever it was
ringing up at three in the morning and doing a lot of
heavy breathing, came crashing through the plateglass
waving a .38.*

*They left a yawning vacuum, gaping holes in the
whole commercial infrastructure you could drive a
tank through if you could find any gas, but Michael
didn't seem to care. He was glad to get them off his
back. He had a big starry vision, a nation in
bushjackets, and if the venal middle-classes didn't like
it, if they weren't prepared to pay their way in the new
democratic socialist Jamaica, then there were five flights
a day to Miami. By the time he was finished, there
were only two . . .*

1976

Michael Manley, the prime minister of Jamaica, was
paying his last respects. A ranking PNP hard-liner had
been shot point-blank. Probably some JLP sportboy
did it, although plenty of people had reason,
considering the guy in the coffin was known to have
a few notches on his gun – that's not a manner of
speaking, that's literally. Apparently this cowboy used
to pull it out wherever he was – at a cocktail party or
a King's House reception for the Cuban hospital
committee – he'd get it out and just oh so
nonchalantly feature the notches on the butt. At one
point he was Michael's chauffeur. So this was a
solemn state occasion.

Michael doesn't show up on the street so much
these days, not like he used to before the bottom fell
out. He can't take the chance. This day, as the funeral
procession wound through the streets of downtown
Kingston, it took a wrong turn; the graffiti changed
from *Seaga Is a CIA Agent!* to *PNP! Assassin!* and
Michael found himself in JLP territory. It was a near
thing. Six of Seaga's sportboys came hauling past in a
hot Cortina shooting everything in sight and the PM
was lucky to escape unscathed.

It's possible, of course, that this is not what
happened. They may have been PNP sportboys in the
car – by what oversight, after all, did the procession
swing right? – it's possible the thing may have been
staged so Michael could blame it on the JLP, if not the
CIA, and get all the *Gleaner* correspondents off his
back, not to mention most of his old friends who've
been giving him a lot of pious libertarian cant on his
proposal for a paramilitary palace guard to protect all
those stupid little party buildings that have been
going up in flames and safeguard the rights of passage
of public figures. Everybody suspects the PNP of
burning their own buildings . . . and so on. Nobody
really knows, so you end up believing everything
you're told and not believing a word anybody says.
What's certain is that the heat's on down here.

You don't hear a lot about it. So far, the government
has done well to keep the lid on. Manley shows up on
the BBC in his sharp bush jacket talking a lot of
dapper radical common sense about the endemic
psychology of *dependence* afflicting the psyche of
any post-colonial society, and the essential need to

direct all that useful energy going bad into something productive and pride enhancing, like digging ditches on the Spanish Town Road. And everybody is disarmed by the amiable high-minded couth of it all. Not until this year, now that Bob Marley's Top Ten, has the word got out and spread. The bottom's fallen out. There's a war on in Jamaica, the government is under siege, and Manley's in the hot seat.

Manley, remember, came to power in his shirt sleeves. He went up into the hills carrying the rod that Selassie had given him – the Rod of Correction he called it – and they flocked to him in jubilant throngs. He wept for them. After ten years of slack JLP government, Manley won in a landslide. His campaign record, "Better Must Come," went to Number One in Jamaica, and he took to the job right away.

There was something a bit ominous about the LP he put out, a kind of sampler of his thinking. And then there was a little white book of resonant pensées and a hardcover called *The Politics of Change*. On the cover was a moody head shot of Manley in shadow, his chin in his hands, his brow furrowed, grappling with the imponderable gravities of post-colonial adolescence, thinking . . . well, the Rastaman out at the beach has a look at that portrait and he says, "It look like Michael write the book, but him not sure if he write the book right. . . ."

That was in 1972, and Manley looked good for a run. He won not only because he milked the aspirations of the dirt poor and downtrodden, he had the support of the money too – he wasn't going to be pushed around anymore by the big bauxite outfits and the hotel owners. He had the right idea about that. And he started wrong. For a while there, if you hit the spot in Jamaica, the word was "bauxite!" That was the charisma of the whole bauxite adventure. Michael staged an OPEC-style face-off on bauxite, the Alcoa and Reynolds board rooms quaked and grumbled and threatened to go to the World Bank, but Michael kept it up, refused to accept arbitration, and the companies started talking about all that bauxite in white Australia. But they've got close to $800 million invested in Jamaica and they gave ground. Manley won a hefty new levy, and the right to see the figures. And just then, the bottom fell out. Aluminium slumped, and it's still slumping. Nobody says "bauxite!" anymore. Now it's "Roots!," "Natty!" or "Ites!," meaning "Higher Heights!" Meaning the Rastas are coming.

Bauxite was the main vein of the economy. And now, now that *Time* and the *Wall Street Journal* and all those freelancers from the weekly magazines have been down, the word's out about the tanks in the streets and the six o'clock curfew and the Gun Court and how you might be woken up at three in the morning with a flashlight in your eyes and a machete at your jugular and some jumpy cowboy full of white rum snarling, *Bloodclooot! Sodomite!*

STRUGGLE. PRODUCE.

Tourism's off as much as 50%. And now most of the tourists are low-rent small fry who come in on an Air Canada charter from Quebec or somewhere and eat all their meals free and spend about $30 in a week, maybe buy a straw hat. The big fry are in the Bahamas. Up in Ocho Rios, Bunny is feeling the pinch. He runs boat trips out of Montego Bay and Ocho Rios, deep-sea fishing trips where as soon as you get out to where they're biting the client is sick from the swell and wants to go home. What Bunny's been thinking about is selling the island off by the square foot. You buy a square foot of beautiful Jamaica for, say, $5 and you get a joke certificate for the rumpus room wall, and all the money would go to buying land and, say, building a playground for the kids. Not all the money; you could put up a playground for around ten grand, and the way Bunny's got it worked out that's only your first 2000 investors.

What's killing Manley – and what may get him killed – is that he hasn't been able to deliver what he promised in the way of creating employment and decolonizing and socializing the economy. His best moves have backfired. His vision of himself at the head of a powerful Caribbean coalition is split down the middle. Trinidad and Barbados are sitting tight on their fattening GNP and buying British, while Guyana's so far gone into delirious doctrinaire Marxist hyperbole, they're all going round calling each other "comrade." Manley remains on the brink, head in hands. Guyana refueled the Cuban airlift to Angola. Barbados refused. Manley, just 90 miles to the south, was saved from playing his last card too fast.

The fact is, the island is just about bankrupt, and a lot of what's left is leaving. Thirty thousand Chinese fled last year. And a great deal of money is going out in stereo cabinets and teddy bears. Food prices are going up fast, unemployment is epidemic, there are sudden shortages. They even ran out of rum for a couple of days before Christmas, another day and it could have gotten really ugly. Macabre, somehow symptomatic ballsups keep happening, like all the poison counter flour that went out this spring. About 20 people died, one father of six took his youngest to hospital, only to see the other five come in and die, one by one.

The reason it may get Manley killed, and killed by one of his own guns, is because it's all gone to his head. His best punches have fallen short. But he's not finished yet. He worked for years in the sugar unions, and he came to power with a vision, a grand missionary design to rescue Jamaica from its rudderless drifting and remake the nation in his own image – like Nyerere did, or Mao, or Castro. A whole nation in bush jackets! He can't stop now. That would betray his manifest destiny, to abdicate the vision to all those venal bludgers in the JLP. From where Manley sits, he has been charged by a higher authority than the fickle affections of the electorate, a kind of historical imperative, clear only to him, to save Jamaica or die trying. So he's digging in. If it means he has to devalue the dollar or suspend the elections, even if it means having to lean on Seaga and the JLP and stir up a bit of burning and looting – he won't stop now.

Down in West Kingston, rival party gangs run the streets. When they collide, and they collide all the time – they can't help it; they're all so wired up and trigger-happy and they're breathing down each other's necks – the whole street goes up. Manley blames it on the CIA. *CIAga,* the smart graffiti say. But not everybody believes him. They're more curious, not to say alarmed, about all the Cubans everywhere. Building schools, building hospitals, nobody seems to know how many of them there are, and the *Gleaner* correspondents and a lot of Michael's old friends who helped him get elected can't see why he's so stoked to have them when half the island's unemployed. There's news in Spanish on the radio. And nobody speaks Spanish in Jamaica.

There have been cabinet resignations. The minister of national resources quit recently, claiming Michael was smitten with Castro and the way he'd put the country to work and accused him of manoeuvring to turn Jamaica into totalitarian communist fiefdom. Michael said forgive the guy, he's cracking up, we've been keeping it a secret – and whoever says they've seen a secret crack corps training in the hills is lying. And they'd better watch out, because he's coming up with a new law, what's called the utterance law, which makes it a felony to make an utterance designed or construed to undermine the elected authority and disbars the felon from ever holding public office. Meantime, Castro is due in Kingston on Labor Day.

The man in the drugstore in Liguanea Plaza has to laugh. He's feeling a certain pressure. He owns the novelty shop opposite, and he just had a customer in there and they were talking about the political vendetta and last night's massacre down in Jones Town where an eyewitness in an upcoming murder trial was shot in his bed, and his son too – he just happened to be there – and the customer says, "You shouldn't be talkin' about all them things. You could get shot." And the shop owner says, "I might as well get shot for something. They're gonna shoot me anyway." And he laughs, a girlish soprano giggle that catches in his throat, his tonsils rebel, his eyes bulge and for a moment he nearly chokes.

Edward Seaga.

44

"Babylon is on a thin wire," says Bongo Moses.
This guy has got the best locks in St Anns. He takes
off his tam and his locks are so plentiful they're all
piled up and coiled on top of his head like rope in
peat and he can polish off a bottle of Dragon in the
time it takes for them to stir and start to slip and
finally unravel to a point below the small of his back
– "These are the Last Days", he says. Bongo Moses,
you must understand, is suffering. He's sitting round
half-naked in the shade of a swaying palm listening
to himself talk, and if he's thirsty he just has to shin
up the nearest tree and chop down a fat green
coconut, better still send a boy to do it, and if he's
hungry he just has to look at a tree and it will bear
fruit while he's watching practically, and if he wants
to flex his brains Jah gave him ganja in abundance to
feed his meditations. If he's feeling fractious, he says,
what he likes to do is swim right out to sea as far as
he can till he's fighting for air and his arms are like
lead and his toes cramp up, and then he sees if he
can get back alive. But Moses doesn't like it here.
He's homesick. He's waiting for the Lion of Judah to
call him home to Zion.

The Rastafarian Brotherhood first sprang up in Jamaica in the thirties, in the wake of Marcus Garvey. Garvey was a messianic Jamaican evangelist who went around Harlem and the south side of Chicago in the twenties prophesying the coronation of a black king in Africa who would redeem the lost tribes of Judah and call them home. Eventually the Americans lost patience with this heretic in their midst, flattering the aspirations of the ghetto vote, and they deported him in 1927. But Garvey was a hard man to stop – all the abuse and ridicule and mute incomprehension he came up against only lubricated his convictions and made him more determined. Back in Jamaica, he went on preaching black pride and African redemption. The polo classes took fright and locked him up for contempt. Worse, the black majority were slow to warm to his theme – his enthusiasm for the simple virtues of thrift and honest toil didn't do much for the pride of the bone-lazy unemployed. He died in England in 1940, disappointed but unrepentant.

In Jamaica today, Garvey is a hero of the state, looming like a latter-day Moses in everybody's imagination. Everywhere you go there's a school named after him, or a park, or a block of flats, he appears on the bank notes, in the spot where the Queen used to be. His career was a long run of flops

and fiascos – but Garvey has had his revenge.

The future of the black man, he said, lies in his past. He must rediscover his African inheritance and seek his culture and his destiny in the great black continent of his ancestors. 'Look to Africa,' he said, 'when a black king shall be crowned, for the day of deliverance is here.'

When Ras Tafari was crowned Emperor Haile Selassi I in Ethiopia in 1930, the King of Kings, Lord of Lords, the Conquering Lion of the Tribes of Judah – when Garvey's followers in Jamaica saw the pictures on the front page of the *Gleaner* they went to their Bibles. To Revelations 5, verses 2, 5 and 6, where it says: 'And I saw a strong Angel proclaiming with a loud voice, "Who is worthy to open the book, and to loose the seals thereof?" . . . And one of the elders sayeth unto me "Weep not: behold, the Lion of the tribe of Judah, the Root of David, hath prevailed to open the book and loose the seven seals thereof. And I beheld, and, lo, in the midst of the throne and of the four beasts, and in the midst of the elders, stood a Lamb as it had been slain, having seven horns and seven eyes, which are the seven spirits of God set forth unto all the earth." ' And later, when Ethiopia fell to the Italians, and pictures appeared in the paper of Selassie standing fast on what they said was an unexploded bomb, they went to Revelations

19, verse 19, where it says: 'And I saw the beast, and the kings of the earth, and their armies, gathered together to make war against him that sat on the horse, and against his army.' And when Selassie returned triumphant to Ethiopia in 1941 they went to the next verse: 'And the beast was taken, and with him the false prophet that wrought miracles before him, with which he deceived them that had received the mark of the beast, and them that worshipped his image. These both were cast alive into a lake of fire burning with brimstone.' And it all became clear. They recognized Selassie as the Lion, the One True God of the prophecy – not God's vicar or His immaculate offspring, but the Living God, Old Alpha himself.

Selassie himself never went so far as to acknowledge his divinity, not in so many words. But the old gnome was perched on the oldest throne in Africa, if not the world, the direct descendent of the legendary issue of King Solomon and the Queen of Sheba, heir to the ancient Ethiopian Empire of all Africa – and in his prime, before he was overtaken by senility and mutiny, Selassie spared nothing and nobody in living up to his legend. He certainly didn't spare the Ethiopians, who died like flies from chronic starvation with the Emperor's name on their lips, while he and his entourage of relatives and libertines spoiled themselves to death in Addis Ababa.

He kept lions in the Palace, great mangy beasts prowling round the garden. They say he slept with them at his feet, and he was canny enough not to deny it. When a Foreign Minister came to call, he often let them loose. He'd toy with them, pull their

HAILE SELASSIE
Emperor of Ethiopia

ears. You can picture him, this tiny ageing gnome, down on the rug in full battledress shoving his little head into the lion's mouth, while Selwyn Lloyd or somebody shifted nervously in his chair and spilt his Pimm's, trying to think of something to say – as if to make the point that what his own people believed, and a lot of the Rastas believe, was true, that he was indeed divine, mightier by far than the mighty king of the jungle. Vain, even childish, but it certainly had more flair than old LBJ taking a table of journalists and staffers into the men's room, there to reduce them to awe and wonderment at the size of his Texas trouser snake.

Selassie never acknowledged his divinity. But nor did he deny it. The Rastas in distant Jamaica recognized what they understood to be the political niceties of his diffidence, and worshipped him whether he liked it or not. They still do, even now he's flown away home. Long before the Army kicked him out and left him to rot, the old gnome had thrust upon him an unimpeachable divinity in the

Rastafarian imagination that ignores the banality of his death, and resides not in his earthly presence but in his image, in The Word, in the single syllable *Jah*. 'Lion!' they shout, and just calling his name resurrects him. '*Jah* lives,' says Bob Marley and what he means is in the beginning was The Word and The Word was *Jah*. In life, the Rastafarians worshipped and adored him with such ferocity that even he must've gone weak at the knees, when he flew into Kingston on a state visit in the sixties and the brethren turned out in force. They came from all over the island, the Rastas up in the hills walked for a week to get there, and by the time the plane landed and the multitudes caught sight of the Lion painted on the side, they got themselves into such a state that the Emperor refused to get off the plane. He took one look at them, these wild demented creatures, barefoot and half naked, strewn all over the tarmac in various stages of epileptic euphoria, and he went back in. He didn't come out for an hour.

What the Rastas say they want is simple enough. They want to go home. Back to ancestral Africa, where they belong. Back to Zion, before the Rivers of Babylon burst their banks and the earth opens up and the whole godless white civilization goes up in flames, as it surely will, according to prophecy. 1960, Garvey had said, was the date for the launch of the great repatriation, but the Rastas are not disheartened by the delay. They wait, as they have waited all their lives and will probably always wait, up in the scrub and down in the rising stench of the shantytowns of West Kingston, for the Emperor to call them home. That was never likely; now of course it would take a miracle and they know it. But that is immaterial. Ethiopia is a *promise*.

There have been false starts. Back in the 50's a Rasta called Prince Edward C. Edwards advertised a great convention of the brethren behind the Tivoli Cinema in Kingston Pen. Rastamen from all over the island dropped everything, gave away their last possessions because they wouldn't need them anymore, and came to town expecting to go on board. Down behind the Tivoli, huge stinking piles of old tyres burned day in and day out, the *akete* drums never let up, the Niyamen danced till their legs gave out and still they staggered, and whoever felt the spirit quickening in him like a rabies took the stands and testified till he blacked out and another took his place. It went on for twenty-eight days. When it was over, there were no ships at the pier.

Until the ships come in, and they know they won't, they will suffer. They won't starve – nobody starves in Jamaica, it's an island of farmers. Even down in Trench Town you can pick your lunch off a bread-fruit tree in somebody's yard and most times he won't mind. Another day he might come after you with a machete, but that's the chance you take. The devout Rastas anyway aspire to a strict Nazarene code of conduct. They don't drink – if it's a hot day and they've got a terrible thirst they might wet their lips with a Red Stripe, they might take a taste of rum here and there when they're feeling low – but they don't drink, and they don't eat meat. They don't beg and they don't steal. They live in random vagrant communities down in shantytown and up in the scrub, trusting in God's grace and the healing powers of the sacramental weed to grant them peace and understanding, that they may be acceptable in His sight. And they suffer. Suffering is what the Rastafarian solution is all about.

It takes a while to get the hang of it because they spend most of their waking life on the point of vanishing into delirious metaphor, and the weird apocalyptic algebra of Rasta revelation only makes sense when you smoke a pound and a half of ganja a week and abandon all reason. Then it seems simple. The Rastas take it from the Bible that they are the true Jews of the prophecy, buried alive in a hostile

and godless white society that couldn't care less about the black man down at the bottom of the heap. They never wanted to come here and they don't want to stay. So they take no part. They have disenfranchised themselves. They don't vote, they don't pay taxes or contribute in any way, because they renounce their citizenship and recognize no authority but the Emperor, wherever he may be, whenever his resurrection may come. They have defected body and soul from Jamaican society into an outcast astral identity beyond the law.

It's immaterial that Ethiopia is just somewhere over the rainbow. A lot of them don't even know where it is. They'll never live to plant a kiss on the deserts of their ancestors. But that's immaterial too. What Rasta offers is the promise of redemption. And when you're down in the dirt and you feel like you've been down in the dirt for four hundred years and you're worse off than ever, it's a solution. Rasta is not just some half-witted heretic sect selling space in the hereafter. It's an alternative spiritual nationality.

The revelation goes on for days and nights, but there is no Rasta Church. There are the odd backyard cells with an outhouse daubed in Ethiopian red, green and gold, a few big crude maps and diagrams on the fence showing the distribution of the races in the world and a few yellowed snapshots of Selassie. There are transient maildrops for international Ethiopian efforts like the Mystic Masons and the Coptic Church. But there is no priesthood, no clergy, no ceremonial. There isn't even a consensus of belief. If they are fools, they are holy fools, and they can always penetrate another layer of subtle scriptural sub-plot and reinvent the prophecy, not just to satisfy their doubts, because they don't have doubts, but actually to reinforce their revelation.

Consider the Duke of Gloucester. He wandered off into the desert, they say, nibbling grass, where he discovered that he was the reincarnation of Nebuchadnezzar, the last King of Babylon, whose chosen task it was to abdicate the throne so as later to succeed the reincarnation of Elizabeth I and preside over the utter destruction of Babylon. It's no good saying wait a minute, what Duke of Gloucester, that was the Prince of Wales – in the gospel according to Bongo Moses the names change, facts are fluid, the point of departure here is that young Edward presented Selassie with a Something like that, the point of departure here being that young Edward presented Selassie with a

60

sceptre at the coronation, which is true, and that sceptre was the sceptre of the ancient Ethiopian Empire of all Africa, the very one, stolen by Imperial Rome, and stolen from Rome by Britain and at last returned to the Lion in recognition of his manifest divinity. In return, they say, Selassie sent George V an emblem. And the emblem, when he received it, cut the old King down, he was stricken by a sudden paralysis and all the efforts of the finest medical minds in Babylon could not undo the unfathomable hex, and he died. . . .

This is not widely known. This is actually known only to a few enlightened Rastamen who got it from another Rastaman they met somewhere, and God knows where he got it from. From the Bible, in fact, according to an invisible code – a kind of hallucinatory X-ray which deciphers the subtext and unravels the metaphor and reveals whatever suits them, hidden beneath the evil blasphemies and lies that every Rastaman knows in his bones are forgeries planted by craven white ecclesiastics in the pay of the Pope in an attempt to confuse the black man and obscure the prophecy. They've all got some personal angle on the prophecy they've cooked up on the strength of a little learning and a lot of days and nights spent sitting around in a backyard somewhere working on a pound and a half of ganja and debating the scriptural imponderables, which is the way they spend most of their time.

When they get going full rev, when they really get their teeth into something – like what's the difference between their claim to their ancestral identity and the white Jamaican's claim to his? And what's more, why should a Rastaman lift a finger to participate in a society that thinks he's just some poor dope-fiend with fried spinach for brains? – anything like that, deep and fraught with metaphor, so they can work up some pace, the Rastas make the Ancient Mariner sound like a man of few words. They hit cadenzas of maniacal rhetoric that are so fluid and have such sheer velocity, such sheer lyric genius, that eventually your earthbound linear systems pack up, your eyes swim, your brains turn to spinach, your tongue feels like a lizard in your mouth, and as they go further and deeper into delirious metaphor, you begin to realize that the Rastas are the conscience of the island.

And there's more and more of them. Jamaica is in the grip of Rasta *crise*. Down in the Jungle, the Rude Boys are growing locks and defecting in droves into outcast astral Ethiopianism. And not just the kung-fu kids, but also what's left of the middle-classes. Prominent heiresses, your *nouveau noire* Rasta intellectuals in the Twelve Tribes of Judah, Bob's mob, people Michael went to Jamaica College with are coming round to the view that what they long ago

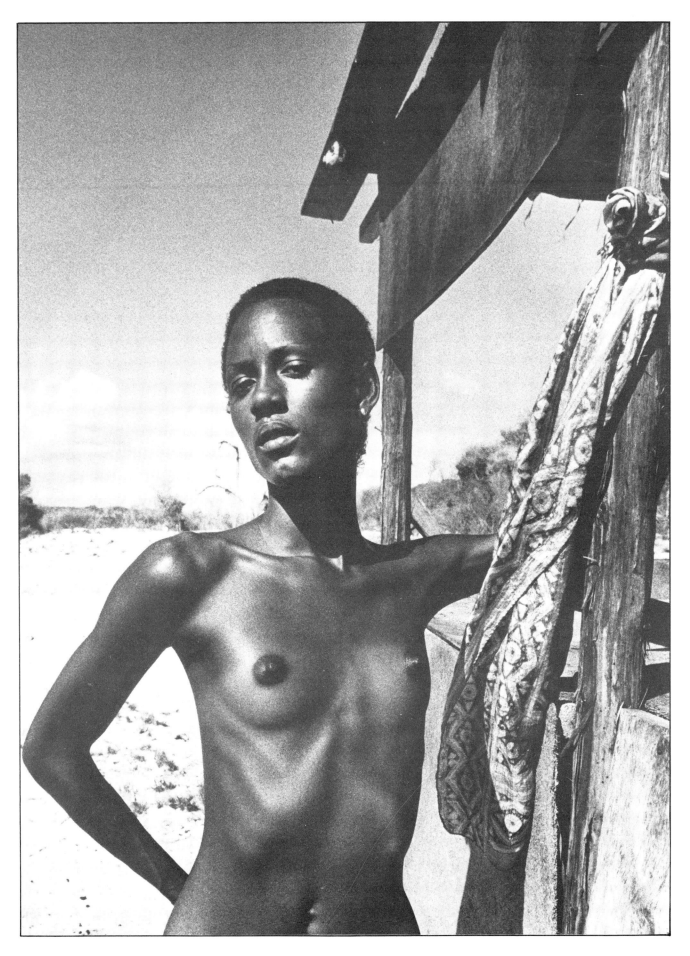

suspected is true. The Rastas are right. The only position to take on a small agricultural island famous for the most effortless narcotic in the world is sitting around all day smoking herb and talking in tongues and let it all fall down. Maybe water the yams, weed the dasheen, milk the goat. Better than going up and down in an elevator . . .

You see a lot of little stickers up on walls saying Coptic Times. There's even a newspaper. They're a secretive bunch, with reason, but they're organised. The passive pariah posture has been overtaken by events. The Coptics are the closest thing there's ever likely to be to a Rasta party.

They started out in a small way in St Elizabeth's.

They were ascetics, they didn't grow locks, and they kept out of harm's way on little fairytale farms up in the hills with a little white picket fence and two goats, two pigs, two chickens, two of everything, like the Ark. Then they started buying land. Not just a couple of acres next door, they started buying parcels of land all over the island, for cash, in US dollars, choice farming land. They weren't just planting out a little herb to feed their meditations, they were in the wholesale side, they had brethren all over the island cultivating vast panoramas of the stuff. By the time they moved to St Thomas they had outgrown the picket fence, they put up chainlink instead, and they had two powerful speedboats out in the bay.

I head rest with Jah. Bob Marley is sitting round
with Family Man and Carly and a bunch of natty
Tuff Gong stragglers in the studio at Hope Rd. They're
meant to be putting down some tracks but it takes
a while to get into the spirit of the thing and so
far all that's happening is Bob and Family Man
are hard at work on a spliff the size of a snocone –
bigger, like a huge smouldering turnip – and
they're falling all over each other, jabbing each
other in the belly, and Bob keeps saying *I head rest
with Jah.* This old-time has-been from the radio
station is hanging around the edges, trying to muscle
in on the spliff, and he asks Bob if he minds if he
watches him do the record. And Bob says no, he
doesn't want him standing round *watching* him, and
the old deejay says, well he didn't mean that, he
didn't mean stare at him, and Bob says look here . . .

'It look like you want to find out where I head rest.
You goin' round all kind of corner tryin' for smart me
to find out where I head rest. But if you want to find
out where I head rest, just come and ask me where I
head rest. If you want to know where I head rest, I
head rest with *Jah.*'

56 Hope Road used to be the local offices of Island Records, but now he's top ten in Babylon, Bob's taken it over. There've been some changes made. Before, it was a big pink colonial job. Now it's dayglo Ethiopian. The walls are covered with teeming African cosmologies and Rasta hieroglyphics depicting the eternal flame and the thrusting seed and much much more. It's got a big wall round it, and the yard's full of eponymous BMW's, red ones, green ones, gold ones. There's a storefront selling Tuff Gong records and girls selling I-tal food and on a good night there are fifty or sixty people hanging round the yard smoking herbs and contemplating the fall of Babylon. Herbs are legal here. Bob's so big, so powerful, he's untouchable. 56 Hope Road's uptown, it's within mortar range of King's House, where Michael Manley lives, and no policeman would be fool enough to set foot in the place in anger.

Bob's in the kitchen, eating a grapefruit. The Wailers are out the back, working on a tune, and Bob's in the kitchen talking to Don Taylor, the Wailers' manager. Don says let me try some of that grapefruit, he leans forward to reach it – blam! The door slams open and a skinny kid in a black leather jacket closes his eyes and lets fly with a submachine gun. Don Taylor was shot six times in the back. Bob was winged. This is less than a couple of weeks before the election of 1976.

Rumours flew like bats. There was a school of thought on the sidelines that swore blind it wasn't a political shooting at all, it had to do with a murky deal out at the racetrack that came unstuck. But the background was this: Bob wanted to put on some concerts. He was rehearsing that night for the first one in George the Fifth Park in a few days time. (It's not called George the Fifth Park any more of course, it's called Independence Park or something meaningful

like that, but everybody still calls it George the Fifth.) He'd suggested these free concerts, and the government of course had jumped at it. They offered to lay things on, venues and transport and so on. What they really wanted was Bob's endorsement. This was the first election eighteen-year-olds could vote, and if Bob was to endorse the PNP then the tide would turn Michael's way. But Bob wasn't crazy. He refused. Then they'd come up with the idea the first concert could be right on Michael's doorstep, on the lawn at King's House, but that was a bit too handy and Bob had it moved to George the Fifth or whatever it's called. Not bad, it's in Manley's constituency. The JLP boys knew a coup when they saw one, they got desperate and somebody shot him. That's the widely held view.

There is a further, more sinister view that says the PNP boys panicked. What if Bob got up on stage and said – now Jamaica was in the grip of intense Rasta crise, remember, every hustler in Kingston was Rasta overnight, Rasta was the power in the land and Bob was the Voice of Rasta, what if he got up and said Rasta don't vote!?!? That would be a bodyblow. So the PNP boys got the wind up and they shot him. God only knows. All he saw was a pair of black leather gloves holding a machine gun. There were fifty or sixty people at Hope Road that night, and seven or eight gunmen who came and went in two white Toyotas, the brave boy with the machine gun went for Bob, and his chums fired into the crowd, Bob's wife got shot in the head, just grazed – and the odd thing is nobody ever saw any of those boys again.

Michael rushed to his bedside. And when Bob got up a couple of days later and did the show, still strapped up in bandages, Michael jumped up on stage

with him, put his arm round him and so on – and it made a powerful impression on the brethren.

Then, late in the day, the JLP were in conference in Montego Bay and somebody said they had a smoking gun. They'd come up with a PNP gunman with a story to tell and a gun they could trace to party headquarters clinching proof of what everybody knew anyway. The police galvanised themselves and made an arrest. He was an ex-army character. And when they looked in his briefcase they struck gold. Incontrovertible documentary evidence of a plot to overthrow the government! This ex-army character swore on his mother's life he'd never seen any of this stuff before, but you'd expect him to say that. This was gold dust. A CIA plot! The government acted swiftly to save the nation. They declared a state of emergency, rounded up a couple of hundred JLP insiders, locked up half the opposition on the eve of the vote, and while Michael was scrupulous, while he made it clear he couldn't exactly prove the CIA were plotting to get rid of him like they got rid of Allende, not prove it in court, he found it difficult to come to any other conclusion, everything pointed that way, the way the Daily Gleaner was being cunningly manipulated irresistibly recalled what the papers did to Allende in Chile – and so on. The first CIAga graffiti caught on. And Manley won by a distance.

Walking down the road with the pistol in your waist,
Johnny you're too bad.
Walking down the road with the machete in your waist,
Johnny you're too bad.
Just a-robbing and a-stabbing, and a-looting and a-shooting,
You know you're too bad.
One of these days you may hear a voice say, come.
Where you gonna run to?
You're gonna run to the law for rest, where there will be no more run.

Slickers

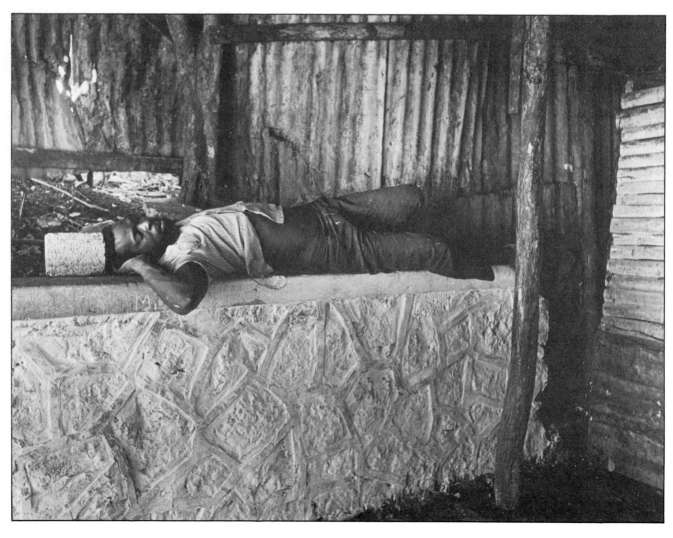

Bob Marley and Claudie Massop.

1978

There's a kind of a hush. Claudius Massop from Tivoli Gardens and Bucky Marshall from Kingston Pen walked up to each other in the street and swore to stop trying to kill each other and burn each other up, because they'd come round to the point of view there wasn't much future in it. The battle had been bloody. Bucky's PNP boys had powered in hard and wiped out a lot of Massop's JLP boys, and not just nohopers, they got a few ranking party members as well – and Massop's boys had come back with a vengeance late in the day and massacred entire households of PNP supporters, until it seemed like there was no stopping the epidemic of political violence and nobody even tried very hard, and it seemed likely the whole island was going to go up in flames the way the Twelve Tribes of Judah insist it must. It came close. The elections of late 76 *were* a civil war in Jamaica, the nation was at its own throat, and it ran on into 77, the year Marcus Garvey predicted all hell would break loose. But Michael Manley won, handsomely. He won by the most incredible landslide in Jamaican parliamentary history. Even the bruised JLP hardliners admit that even

allowing for all the dead people who voted ten times and the PNP torpedoes who went round picking up any JLP electoral supervisor and putting him out of action for the days it took to count the ballot, even allowing for that, Michael pulled a coup. He got through with his charisma intact, and the JLP were smashed. He's there to stay now, free to reinvent the nation and implement his grand design, if he's got one.

So the violence has run out of steam. Which doesn't mean that just because Massop and Bucky shook hands and Manley and Eddie Seaga stood side by side in the rain at Bustamante's funeral and the nation reunited, for a day, in grief – it doesn't mean there are not plenty of kung fu kids in mirrored shades running round West Kingston living dangerously, looting and shooting and even last year kidnapping school kids. There are so many guns in Jamaica, and so many idle hands. The old party line resentments have not gone away, but they have been starved for ammo. There is now an *acceptable* murder rate.

What's happening now is people are lying low, waiting to see what's going to happen next. They

L. to R.: The Bishop of Jamaica, Edward Seaga's mother, Seaga, Governor General Florizel Glasspole and Mrs. Glasspole.

know something's got to happen because things
can't go on like they are with no rice in the shops, no
Red Stripe for Christmas, no sugar, no schoolbooks,
cars broken down all over the island and no parts
since the import ban. The foreign exchange window
at the Bank of Jamaica is closed and the dollar's
down 40% in a year. The fugitives, up in Miami, are
looking good – even if they find Florida just a little
banal, bland, numbingly boring in fact. People can
only wait and see and speculate. There's a story you
can't miss about Castro coming down on Labor Day
more or less unannounced and telling Manley if he
didn't want to spend the rest of his life eaten alive by
ulcers he should steer clear of the Russians, he'd
been dealing with the assholes for nearly twenty
years and if he had his way what he'd really like to
do is get them off his phone and deal with America,
some sweet old sucker like George McGovern.
Scandalous stuff, and the way Fidel's been ploughing
his new bionic army into the Ogaden alongside the
Russians and spreading napalm all over Zion hardly
seems calculated to melt the ice in Washington. All
the same, the Cuban adventure in Jamaica remains
on hold, in uneasy abeyance. The tireless doctors are
still all over the place, and you can see plenty of
healthy specimens at the airport drinking double
Scotches and glowing with unnatural confidence,
flashing brilliant state-owned teeth. But Manley
remains as ambiguous as ever. His initial heavy crush
on Fidel appears to have wilted a little, and he's
looking around for alternative input. He's even
stopped badmouthing the multinationals.

The way one of Claudie's boys put it, *Fidel is a good man in his own field* – but that brand of regimental ideological programming just can't work in an island of feckless anarchists and visionaries. If Castro had only lingered long enough at the jukebox, he might have realised he was on a hiding to nothing. You just can't preach godless uniformity in the national interest to people with no interest in the national interest for the very reason that they know for an unflinchable fact they have been chosen by the Creator to witness the fall of Babylon and all its works any day now, and when that happens, only the Rastas will be saved because they alone defend truth and rights and consequently reject any system at all on the grounds that systems are by definition unholy and oppressive and that includes communism or democratic socialism or whatever you want to call it. So far the moment of decision has proved indecisive. Castro was oddly subdued – he only spoke for about three and a half hours. They listened for a while. But he wasn't so hot. He bombed. All that overwrought Latin *angst* never stood a chance against Big Youth.

Claudie and Bucky had big plans. They actually signed a Peace Treaty. Everybody held their breath. It was crazy, but it was symptomatic. It was rule by charisma. It was what Manley did. But his was wearing thin. And here you had two brassy thugs from the Jungle giving the orders, holding press

conferences, telling everybody what they should do, and nobody had the heart to stop them. A few months back, Claudie Massop didn't have a bicycle. Overnight practically he's driving a BMW, he's got a string of horses in training out at Caymanas Park, and he and Bucky can do no wrong. They put together a big concert to bless their alliance. Claudie got the Wailers to come back down to Kingston to close the show, and that took some charisma on its own, Bob hadn't been seen much since the shooting. It all came to an ecstatic finale when Manley and Seaga appeared on stage together and Bob held their hands aloft, locked in brotherly love. Peter Tosh gave Michael a spliff. For one long balmy weekend, peace broke out.

A few weeks later, Claudie and Bucky were dead, Bob was dying, and the real estate man out in Portland stands frowning at his fishpond. His son has emptied a can of expensive gasoline into the water and the fish are suffering. They haven't got long to live. A couple of rare silver Samoan sticklebacks are already floating on top. Sadly, he pulls his .38 out of his special holster he got in Miami that lodges somewhere in his groin. But he hesitates. This is the question. This is what's driving him crazy in Jamaica in 1978. Should he blast the Samoan sticklebacks and put them out of their agony. Or, bullets being in short supply, should he hold his fire and let them stiffen slowly, in case he has to shoot a man tonight.

The election of 1980 was a killer. Michael was on the ropes by then, he was weaving on his feet, punchy with disappointment – he could see it all slipping through his fingers and he'd run out of ideas. The grand design shot to pieces. And the tragedy of it, what did him in, was this: it wasn't his fault. He'd led the nation to chaos and ruin and let loose a bloodbath nobody could handle but it wasn't really his fault. He was the victim of cruel twists of fate, the worldwide rehearsal for the collapse of capitalism, more than once he tried the right move at the wrong time like the bauxite mess. Worst of all, what he never really understood, he was trying to run a country that just wouldn't listen.

At the end, as bankruptcy stared him in the face and the last chance he had was the IMF, he cut his own throat. He took exception to the way they were treating him, all these ulcerous little accountants acting like he was some kind of unstable amateur – and he kicked them out. You could hear the bells toll.

In between the snap and crackle of small arms fire and the hammer of the machine guns and the nagging racket of the helicopters overhead, all day on election day you could hear the bells toll all over Kingston. For Whom the Bell Tolls was the JLP slogan. Michael bit the dust.

*These days, in Jamaica, the Rasta crise is past. It all
went a bit haywire. The Coptics got busted, the nouveau
noire Rasta theologians got ringworm, Bob Marley died.*

*There are more militant locksmen powering round
Brixton and Birmingham, where the Rasta solution
makes more sense to the futureless black unemployed
jammed into neglect in Thatcher's Britain than it does
to the lounging locksmen in Eddie Seaga's post-
apocalyptic island in the sun. The Manley Years are
over. The dust is settling. The apocalypse is blown out.
Somewhere, Michael sits staring at the hummingbirds
annoying his bougainvillea, licking his wounds.
Thinking about that flat tyre –*

*There was a joke going round at the height of
Manley's last desperate gamble with destiny when he
kicked out the IMF, there was this joke: Michael's
BMW has a flat tyre. He gets out, jacks it up, changes
the tyre, reaches for the nuts to secure the spare – and
he knocks the hubcap and they all spill down the
drain. He scratches his head. No big thing, says a
voice. He's stopped outside the madhouse, and he
turns to find a madman watching him through the
railings. A Rastaman. All you must do is take one nut
from the other three wheels, he says. Simple as that.
So Michael does what he says, secures the tyre, thanks
him, opens the door – and then he pauses. He has to
ask. What's a man as smart as you doing in the
madhouse? The Rastaman shrugs. I mad, y'know.
Not foolish.*